# USBORNE
# Young Puzzle Adventures

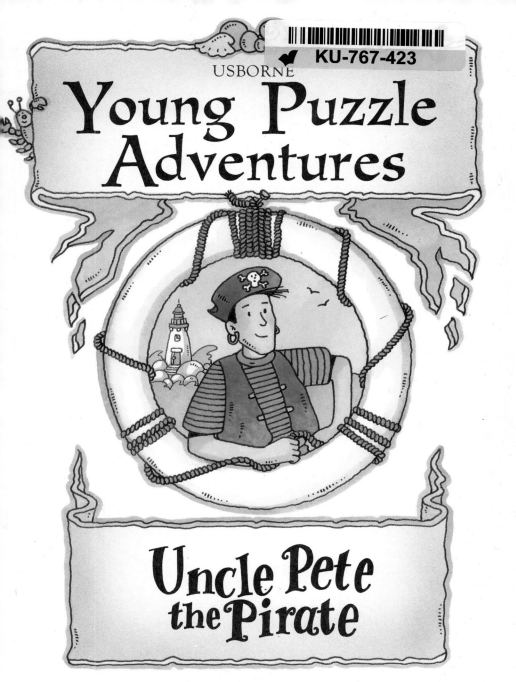

# Uncle Pete the Pirate

Susannah Leigh

Designed and Illustrated by Brenda Haw

Series editor: Gaby Waters    Assistant editor: Michelle Bates

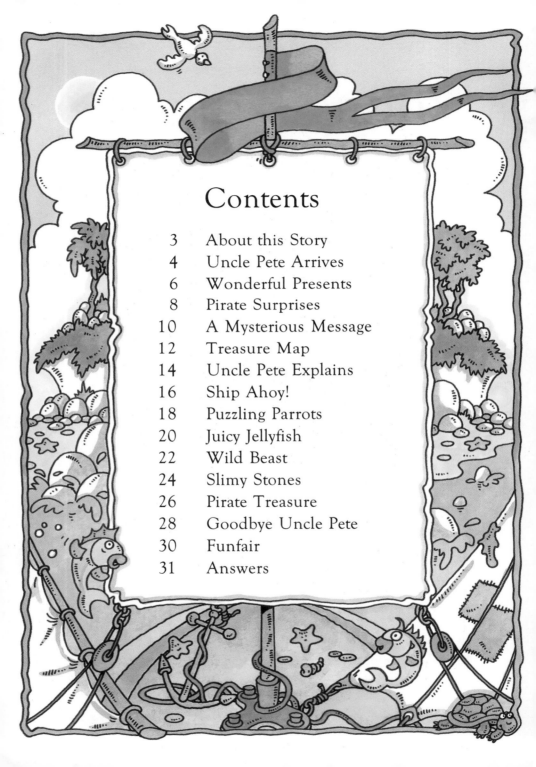

# Contents

# About this Story

MARY

UNCLE PETE

Keep your eyes open for clues. If you get stuck, there are answers on pages 31 and 32.

When this story begins, Mary is looking forward to her Uncle Pete the pirate, coming to visit. Uncle Pete comes home once a year and this time he has the most amazing pirate adventure in store for Mary. Just turn the page to find out more...

# Uncle Pete Arrives

On the day Uncle Pete came to visit, Mary raced down to the little port near her house where she had promised to meet him. Mary couldn't wait to see Uncle Pete again. She wondered if he would be wearing his blue pirate hat. He was sure to have some pirate tales to tell, if only she could find him.

**Can you see Uncle Pete?**

Funfair Today

# Wonderful Presents

Mary ran over to the little café where Uncle Pete sat waiting, sipping a glass of pirate punch. When he saw Mary he jumped up and gave her a big hug. Mary was very happy to see Uncle Pete and especially excited to see the wonderful presents he had brought her. They were laid out on a pink cloth on the table. Mary wondered where Uncle Pete had found them all.

"Your presents came from the friends I made during my adventures at sea," he said.

Uncle Pete told Mary about all the fantastic places he had been to and all the amazing things he had seen on his pirate journey. His story was so real, she could picture him sailing across the ocean. She could even guess exactly where each of her presents came from.

**Can you guess where Uncle Pete found each of Mary's presents?**

# Pirate Surprises

Uncle Pete and Mary walked back up the road to Mary's house.

"I hope you won't be bored, Uncle Pete," Mary sighed. "Nothing piratey ever happens here."

Uncle Pete just smiled. He was sure Mary was in for a surprise.

"I think your house is a pirate's playground,
Mary," he said. "Look closely and see for yourself."
Mary rubbed her eyes. She gasped with delight. She
rubbed her eyes again, but there was no mistake.
Today her house looked very piratey indeed.

**Can you spot any pirate things at Mary's house?**

# A Mysterious Message

Mary shivered with excitement and grinned at Uncle Pete. She had a feeling a pirate adventure was just around the corner. She was even more sure when they stepped inside the house and Uncle Pete handed her a postcard. "I found this on the doorstep, Mary," he said. "It's addressed to you. It seems to be some sort of picture message. I wonder what it says."

**What does the card tell Mary to do?**

Dear Mary
go to this 🗃
and find a 📜
from a well-wisher ☠

Dear
gone
will look
after you
love

11

# Treasure Map

This map belongs to Bad Luck Barry
who stole a chest of treasure rare.
That chest was full and hard to carry,
so Barry hid it  over there.

"Over there? Where's that? Please tell."
One picture on this map will show
Barry, burying that treasure well.
Where's it hidden? Do you know?

Saucepan Island

School House

Aunty Brenda's House

Sand castle Island

Puppy Island

Sure enough, on top of the chest, Mary found a rolled up
piece of paper. She spread it out. It had pictures and a
short poem written on it. Uncle Pete read the poem and
gave a great shout.

"Shivering shipwrecks, Mary!" he cried. "This is a
treasure map. It belongs to the pirate Bad Luck Barry."

A pirate's treasure map! Mary could hardly
believe it. Eagerly she read Barry's poem. She
looked at the pictures and caught her breath.
"Uncle Pete," she exclaimed. "I can see where
Barry buried the treasure!"
**Can you see where the treasure is buried?**

# Uncle Pete Explains

The map showed Bad Luck Barry burying the treasure on Lawnmower Island. But Mary was still puzzled. There were lots of things she didn't understand. Who WAS Bad Luck Barry? Where was Lawnmower Island? And what was the treasure buried there? Uncle Pete explained.

Bad Luck Barry is my oldest pirate enemy.

He stole my precious treasure chest.

Then he hid it on Lawnmower Island, which isn't far from here. We must watch out for Barry. He may be very near...

Mary shivered. What an exciting story! She wondered where Barry could be now.

**Can you see him?**

15

# Ship Ahoy!

"When Barry realizes his map is missing, he will be very angry," said Uncle Pete. "We must sail to Lawnmower Island and find my treasure, but first we'll need a pirate boat. Let's see if we can spot one from your roof, Mary."

16

They scrambled up the ladder to the roof where they could see for miles around. Mary looked down over the large garden. "I can see a perfect boat, Uncle Pete," she cried.

**Can you see what Mary and Uncle Pete can use as a pirate boat?**

# Puzzling Parrots

Mary and Pete jumped aboard
their pirate boat and
set sail.

They passed fields
and trees, cows who said
"moo" and fish who flew.

Mary saw other pirates
. . . and waved to friends.
All of a sudden, two pirate
parrots on perches squawked
out a message in rhyme.

You're on the right trail,
but how do we know?
Some things have been pointing
the right way to go.
On Lawnmower Island these
same things will tell,
the way to the treasure,
so follow them well.

Mary giggled. How funny to hear
parrots talking. She scratched her head and
wondered what their strange message meant.

**What things have been pointing the way
on the river journey?**

19

# Juicy Jellyfish

Uncle Pete peered through his treasure-hunting telescope.
"Land Ahoy!" he said. "Drop anchor, Mary. Lawnmower
Island is dead ahead."

Lawnmower Island! Mary quivered with excitement.
Would they really find the treasure here? Uncle Pete tied up
the boat and Mary splashed through the shallow water.
Almost at once she saw the blue arrow that pointed them to
the right path. Mary ran toward the island's soft warm sand
when a shout from Uncle Pete stopped her.

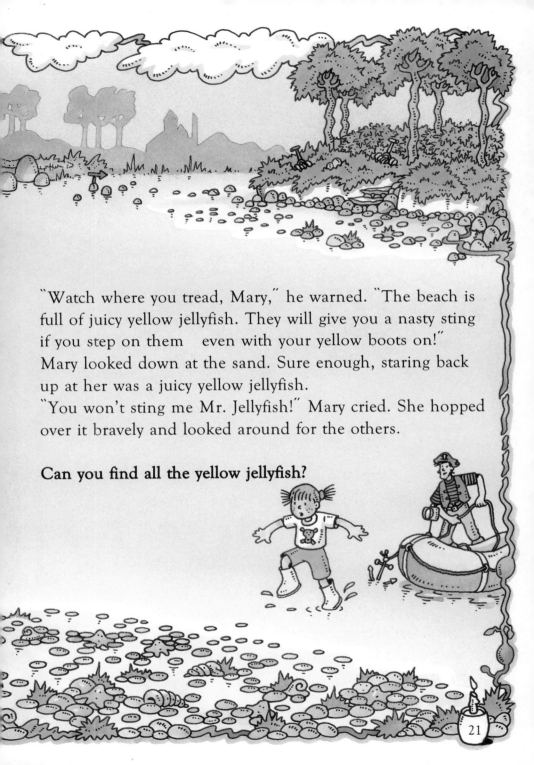

"Watch where you tread, Mary," he warned. "The beach is full of juicy yellow jellyfish. They will give you a nasty sting if you step on them   even with your yellow boots on!" Mary looked down at the sand. Sure enough, staring back up at her was a juicy yellow jellyfish.

"You won't sting me Mr. Jellyfish!" Mary cried. She hopped over it bravely and looked around for the others.

**Can you find all the yellow jellyfish?**

# Wild Beast!

Mary and Pete skipped past the last yellow jellyfish and followed the blue arrow that pointed them deeper into the dark and tangled jungle and closer to Uncle Pete's lost treasure.

Mary looked back to make sure that Uncle Pete was following close behind, when a loud roar stopped her in her tracks. Mary gulped and turned around slowly. She found herself face to face with a large, hairy beast. It had very sharp teeth and big ears.

"Fiery fishtales, Mary!" cried Uncle Pete. "It's the wild beast of Lawnmower Island. If we can find some tasty bones to feed it with, we will be able to sneak past it safely."

**Can you find seven bones for the wild beast to munch?**

23

# Slimy Stones

The wild beast snuffled off with a mouthful of bones. Mary held tightly to Uncle Pete's hand as they continued following the blue arrows across the island. They stopped at a deep pool of water and Pete shook his head. There was no way around. They would have to cross by the stepping stones. Mary sighed. First jellyfish, then a wild beast and now this.

Being a pirate was hard work. You never knew what was just around the corner. But Mary was brave, she wouldn't give up yet. So she jumped from stone to stone, being careful not to tread on the slime and the toads.

**Can you find a way across the stepping stones to the blue arrow on the other side of the water?**

# Pirate Treasure

Mary jumped from the last stepping stone
and crashed on through the jungle. As she turned a
corner she gasped. What do you think she saw? There,
sitting in the middle of Lawnmower Island on a checked
blanket, were her mother and father!

"Surprise, Mary," they cried. "You're almost at the end
of the trail. Take this shovel and dig here for the pirate
treasure."

Mary turned to Uncle Pete who smiled broadly. Mary
grinned and began to dig. Before long she hit something
hard. With Uncle Pete's help, she lifted the object from
the ground. It was a treasure chest.

Inside was the most wonderful pirate picnic Mary had ever seen.

"Eat up Mary," said her dad, brushing the sand from the sandwiches. "And tell us all about your pirate adventures."

Mary was just about to munch on a piece of a pirate pie and tell them all about her exciting time, when she had a terrible thought. Where was Bad Luck Barry? He was sure to be somewhere near and he would want the treasure...

**Bad Luck Barry won't want any treasure and he won't be troubling Mary. Can you see why?**

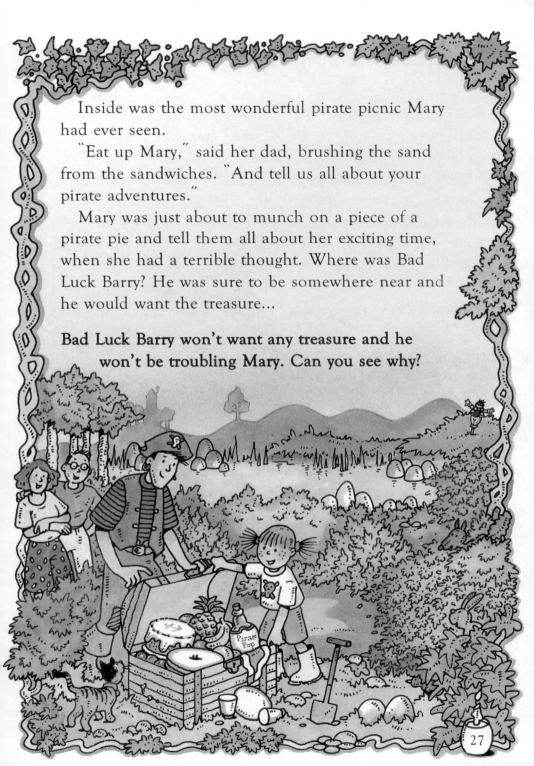

# Goodbye Uncle Pete

After everyone had eaten enough, they sailed back to Mary's house. Then Uncle Pete had to leave. That evening Mary went down to the little port to see him off. She wanted to say one last goodbye and thank him for her marvellous pirate adventure. There was a funfair at the port. But where was Uncle Pete?

**Can you see him?**

GHOST TRAIN

BUGGY RIDE

Have Fun!

FUNFAIR

TODAY ONLY!

BALLS AN
FLUTES — A
EVERY TIM

UNCLE PETE'S PIRATE RIDE

COCONUT SHY

29

# Funfair

"Climb aboard, Mary," Uncle Pete called from the pirate ride. Mary scrambled up and clung on tightly as the merry-go-round whirled and spun. The wind whistled through her hair and music played loudly.

"I'll be back to visit you next year, Mary!" Uncle Pete called above the noise of the fair. "Would you like that?"

Mary thought about her wonderful day. "Oh, yes please, Uncle Pete," she cried. "This has been the best pirate adventure I have ever had!"

# Answers

Uncle Pete has one more puzzle for you. How many lawn mowers can you find on Lawnmower Island?

### Pages 4-5
Uncle Pete is here.

### Pages 6-7
Uncle Pete tells some exciting stories! Here is where Uncle Pete says he found each of Mary's presents. The octopus gave him the flute and the king gave him the cup. The brush belonged to the mermaid and the monkey threw Uncle Pete a coconut. Neptune gave Uncle Pete a listening shell, and the ball is the one the dolphins are playing with.

### Pages 8-9
The pirate things at Mary's house are circled in this picture.

### Pages 10-11
The card tells Mary to go to this chest

and find this map. (Did you spot the other picture message here?) It says: Dear Mary, Gone fishing. Uncle Pete will look after you. Love Ma and Pa.

### Pages 12-13
The treasure is buried on Lawnmower Island. Here is Bad Luck Barry hiding it.

### Pages 14-15
Barry is here.

### Pages 16-17
Mary has spotted a rubber dinghy which they can use as a pirate boat. Here it is.

## Pages 18-19

The blue arrows have been pointing the right way to go. They are circled here.

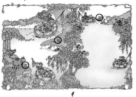

## Pages 20-21

You can see the eleven jellyfish that Mary has to watch out for circled here.

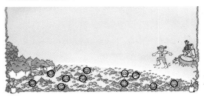

## Pages 22-23

The seven juicy bones are circled here.

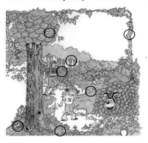

## Pages 24-25

The way across the stepping stones to the blue arrow is marked in black.

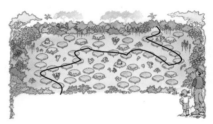

## Pages 26-27

Bad Luck Barry won't want any treasure because he is really a scarecrow! Here he is.

(Did you spot him on page 17 being carried by the farmer?)

## Pages 28-29

Uncle Pete is here. Did you guess?

(Can you see some familiar presents here?)

There are ten lawn mowers on Lawnmower Island.

# MOLLY'S MAGIC CARPET

Emma Fischel
Illustrated by Teri Gower

# Contents

# Meet Molly

This is Molly. She lives by the sea.

Today she is on her way to play. But there is an amazing adventure lying in wait for her. Just follow her outside to find out more.

Keep your eyes open for clues. If you get stuck, there are answers on pages 63 and 64.

# Molly Takes a Tumble

"To the rescue!" shouted Molly, charging down the steps. Today she was a brave knight, off to tame a dragon.

CRASH!

BANG!

WALLOP!

She went tumbling and landed with a big, hard bump.

"Ouch," she said and rubbed her bottom. "That hurt."

"Well, look where you're going next time," grumbled a little voice.

Molly jumped. Who had said that?

"Get your muddy feet off my back. You'll get my pattern dirty. And tie your shoe laces."

Molly was baffled. She looked around her. There was no one outside. But something had spoken to her. Something must be magic.

**What do you think it is?**

# Up, Up and Away!

"You're a talking carpet!" Molly
gasped nearly toppling over.

"A magic carpet," the voice
corrected. "Well . . . almost."

It wriggled.

"The trouble is," it said, "I won't be a real magic carpet
until I do something brave."

The carpet heaved a big sigh. "But I've been flying for
days now and still can't find a single brave thing to do.
And time's running out. Soon I'll become an *ordinary*
carpet ~ no voice, no flying, nothing!"

The carpet curled up at one corner. "Maybe you could
help me," it said.

"I-I'll try," said Molly. And before she knew it, the
carpet lifted off the ground and they were up and away.
Higher and higher they flew, up into the sky.

"Where are we going?" Molly shouted.
"Wonderworld!" cried the carpet. "We
head for the big blue moon, then fly
straight on until breakfast. Hold on tight."

**Here's Molly. Can you help her
find her way to the blue moon?**

# Wonderworld

Wonderworld! What a sight it was!
On and on they flew, over gleaming
oceans and rolling hills, over magical
lands Molly had never even imagined.
They curved and swooped through the sky.
Molly felt light as a feather.

The wind rushed through her hair. The clouds flew by. Soon she felt as though she had been flying forever.

"I never want it to end!" she cried.

The carpet chuckled. "Cloudworld, Spookville, Topsy-turvydom, Monsterland, One Mountain Island, all below us," it sang out.

**Which island do you think is which?**

# Rocky Ride

Just then, the carpet started to jiggle and jitter. Molly clung on for dear life.

"I'm running out of flying magic," the carpet gasped, spinning down toward the sea.

The wave tops came nearer and nearer . . . and so did a very large rock. Molly shut her eyes tight. THUD!

Molly opened her eyes. "We can hop from rock to rock to the beach," she said. "You might be able to," sniffed the carpet. "But not me. I'm far too tired. You'll just have to carry me."

Molly rolled the carpet up carefully, tucking it under her arm. Then someone shouted from the beach.

Watch out!
There is only one safe way to
get here. Don't step on any rocks
with crabs or slimy squids
on them!

**Can you find a safe way to the beach?**

# Safely Ashore

"Made it," gasped Molly, flopping down onto the sand.

"Unroll me, please," a muffled voice squeaked.

"Wow!" said the boy on the beach. "Can that thing really fly?"

"I am not a thing," said a small frosty voice. "I am a carpet. And a very special one at that."

"I beg your pardon," said the boy, eyes popping out of his head as the carpet spoke. "I'm Frank and this is my rabbit. Did you really fly here?"

"All the way," said Molly proudly. "Well almost."

"Can I have a turn?" Frank said eagerly.

"A turn?" the carpet snorted. "I'm not a fairground ride."

"We could fly to the Candy Café," said Frank.

The carpet liked the sound of that. So when it was rested, they set off.

"There it is," said Frank. "It's blue ~ next to the umbrellas."

**Can you spot the Candy Café?**

# A Strange Sight

Bump! The carpet landed. Molly gasped with astonishment. It must be carnival day. There were clowns and stilt walkers, jugglers and acrobats.

Then . . . DONG! An enormous gong boomed out.

What happened next was the strangest thing Molly had ever seen. Everyone stopped moving . . . everyone except Molly. They all froze to the spot like statues.

What was going on? Nobody spoke. Nobody moved. Nobody did anything at all. Then . . . DONG! The gong struck again.

All of a sudden, everyone sprang back into life . . . and into a little trouble.

Molly stood and gaped. "What happened?" she asked Frank. But he didn't answer. He was looking for his rabbit.

**Can you see Frank's rabbit in this picture?**

# Magic Mix~up

"What happened just now is nothing new," sighed Frank. "It happens a lot and it's all the fault of Mort the magician."

Molly listened hard as Frank started to explain . . .

"Mort the magician lives in a castle at the very top of the mountain.

He used to do nice spells. But one day he sent an invitation and all that changed.

Watch me test my latest brilliant spell! Come to the blue lollipop tree at 2 o'clock sharp. Love from Mort

The whole town turned out to watch Mort do his magic.

The magic potion in this jar will turn vegetables into ice cream!

I open the jar, say the magic words . . .

Agga Zagga Doo Doo! And hey presto . . .

But the spell didn't quite do what it was supposed to. Little by little, Mort started to change before our eyes.

Everyone started roaring with laughter. Mort flew into a rage. He hated being laughed at."

I'll make you sorry you laughed at me. Just you wait and see!

**Can you spot all the changes to Mort?**

49

# Molly Has a Plan

"So Mort thought up a brand new spell to pay us back for laughing at him," said Frank, leading the way to the Candy Café. "And now, any time he opens his spell jar, the blue clouds billow out and we all freeze to the spot. It's a dreadful nuisance."

"Can't you stop him somehow?" asked Molly.

"Only by taking the jar with the blue clouds in it," said Frank. "But it's hidden somewhere in his castle. We've tried flying up there . . . but there is nowhere to land. We've tried climbing . . . but he's covered the top in sticky toffee. We've tried everything we can think of . . . nothing works."

**Candy Café - Ices, jellies and lots lots more**

Molly thought hard as Frank finished his story. "There must be a way up," she said. "If the magician does it."

"But he uses magic," said Frank sadly.

"Then so must we," said Molly. "A magic carpet!"

Quick as a flash, the carpet shot off and hid. It didn't like the sound of Molly's idea at all.

**Where is the carpet hiding?**

# Flying High

"This is your big chance, carpet," said Molly, hugging it. "Now you can do something brave!"

"Well, I don't *feel* brave," it said in a wobbly voice. "But I do want to be a real magic carpet. So, let's go!"

"To the top of the mountain!" shouted Molly.

Soon the waving figures on the ground were just tiny specks below them. Molly and the carpet were alone in the big blue sky.

Up and up they flew. Past rivers that plunged into foaming white falls. Past forests of dark, densest green.

The side of the mountain grew steeper and steeper. The clouds rushed past. It grew colder and colder.

And all the while the castle grew closer and closer.

At last the huge castle loomed above them. Three magic birds circled around it, uttering strange harsh cries. Molly listened hard. They seemed to be trying to help her.

**Can you spot the way into the dungeon?**

# Underground

The dungeon was stinky and dark. Slimy things dripped down the walls.

"Which way do we go?" Molly gulped. The carpet just shook like a leaf.

Then Molly saw a map. "This will help us," she said.

**Can you find the way in?**

Way into Castle.

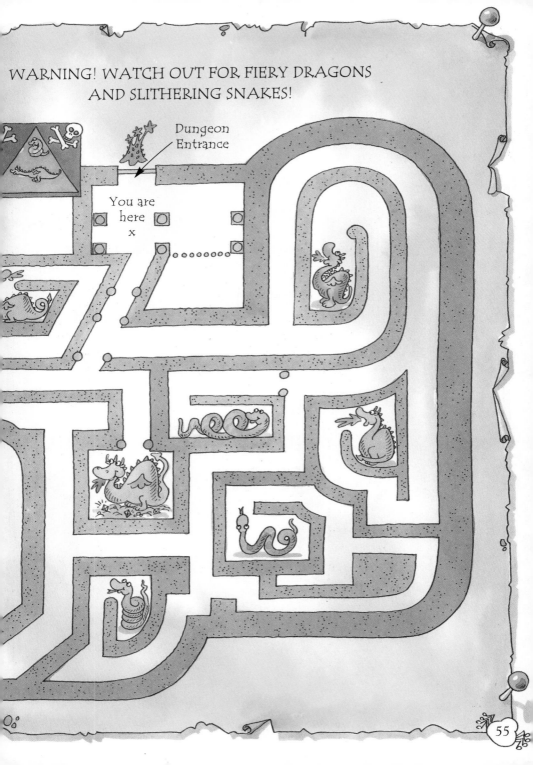

WARNING! WATCH OUT FOR FIERY DRAGONS
AND SLITHERING SNAKES!

Dungeon
Entrance

You are
here
x

# Surprises in Store

"We have to find the spell jar," gasped Molly. Then they whizzed around the castle so fast, it seemed almost as if they were in three places at once.

They tried big doors and small doors . . .

. . . stiff doors

. . . and creaky doors.

Until there was only one place left to look ~ in the highest tower of all.

But there was a shock in store at the top.
Not one magician . . . not two . . . but three!

"Surprise!" they all chortled. "Only one of us is real. But which one? Guess wrong and ~ PLOP! ~ in you go to my pot of stinky slime!"

Then the three magicians started to sing.

The one in stripes of red and blue
Will plop you in the slimy goo
The one in spots of green on blue
Is not the magic man for you
The one with yellow stars you see
Is he you want, you see he's me.

**Can you spot the real Mort?**
**(The song will help you.)**

# The Spell Jar

PFFF! Two of the magicians vanished in a puff of smoke.
Molly and the carpet shot through the door and bolted it.

"You won that time," shouted Mort. "But bolts won't
stop me and if I get to the spell jar first, I shall freeze
everyone to the spot until Christmas!"

"Quick, look for a jar with blue clouds in it," said Molly.

**Can you find the spell jar?**

# Homeward Bound

"Found it!" shrieked Molly. "Let's go!" Leaping onto the carpet, they soared out of the window.

Molly flung the spell jar up in the air. It hung for a moment then down it fell, faster and faster.

SMASH! It hit a rock and splintered into tiny pieces. A puffy blue cloud floated off into the sky.

"Spoilsports!" wailed a faint voice. "I'll never be able to make that spell again. It's gone forever!"

"And a good thing too," shouted Molly.

"Homeward bound," cried the carpet. "Hold on tight. It's a long way down!"

They played hide-and-seek with birds in the clouds.

They raced with shooting stars.

They surfed on the breezes.

They chased waterfalls down the mountainside.

Down and down they flew. And then Molly saw something she recognized. A tree she had noticed before that told her they were near their journey's end.

**Which tree does Molly recognize?**

# Goodbye

"Made it!" gasped the carpet, landing smoothly.

"You brave thing," said Molly, squeezing it. She felt something.

"What's this?" she said. "A label?" She read it carefully . . .

"You've done it!" she said, hugging the carpet tightly. You're a real magic carpet now!"

"Imagine that!" it said, twisting to look at its shiny new label. "I suppose I must be!" And it curled up at one corner with pleasure.

Genuine Magic Carpet

"Then, waving goodbye to Frank and all their new friends, Molly and the carpet set off home. "I wish it didn't have to end," Molly sighed, snuggling down.

"This is only the start," smiled the carpet. "Who knows where we'll go next time!"

# Answers

## Pages 36-37

The magic thing outside is the carpet.
Here it is, right under Molly's feet.

## Pages 38-39

The way to the blue moon is marked here in black.

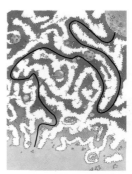

## Pages 40-41

Did you know which island was which? You can see them here.

Monsterland
Topsy-turvydom
Cloudworld
Spookville
One Mountain Island

## Pages 42-43

The safe way to the beach is marked in black. This is the only way that avoids all the crabs and slimy squids.

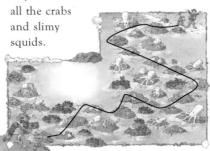

## Pages 44-45

The Candy Café is here.

## Pages 46-47

Frank's rabbit is all tangled up under the carpet. Here he is.

**Pages 48-49**
All of the changes to Mort are circled here.

**Pages 50-51**
The carpet is hiding above the sign for the Candy Café.

**Pages 52-53**
The Ifflediffle plant hides the entrance to the secret passage. It is circled below.

**Pages 54-55**
The way into the castle is marked in black.

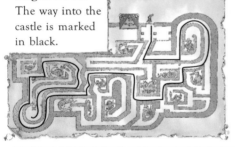

**Pages 56-57**
The real Mort is the one with yellow stars on his magician's coat. He is in the middle.

**Pages 58-59**
Here is the spell jar.

**Pages 60-61**
Molly recognizes the blue lollipop tree. She knows it means she is nearly back at the town.

# Lucy
## and the
# Sea Monster

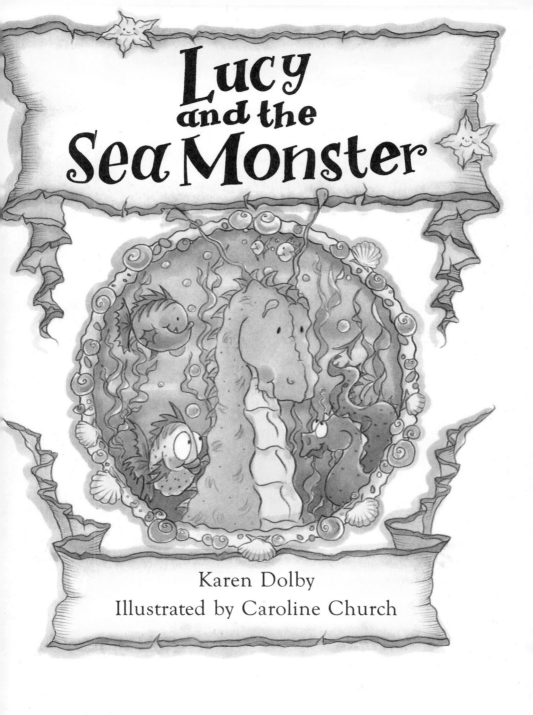

Karen Dolby
Illustrated by Caroline Church

# Contents

# About this Story

This story is about Lucy and Tom Cat. They are on their way to the beach where their amazing adventure begins

LUCY

TOM CAT

Keep your eyes open for clues. If you get stuck there are answers on pages 95 and 96.

Turn the page for a great adventure.

# On the Beach

Lucy sat on a rock on the beach, reading a fantastic adventure story about dragons and monsters. Tom Cat was nearby watching fish jump.

Waves lapped against Lucy's rock and crashed onto the shore. Her tummy rumbled. It was nearly supper time.

Tom Cat yowled as a wave washed over him. Lucy looked up. She couldn't see anything. But there was something that Lucy had not spotted. It was in the water, coming closer and closer.

**Look at the opposite page. Can you see what it is?**

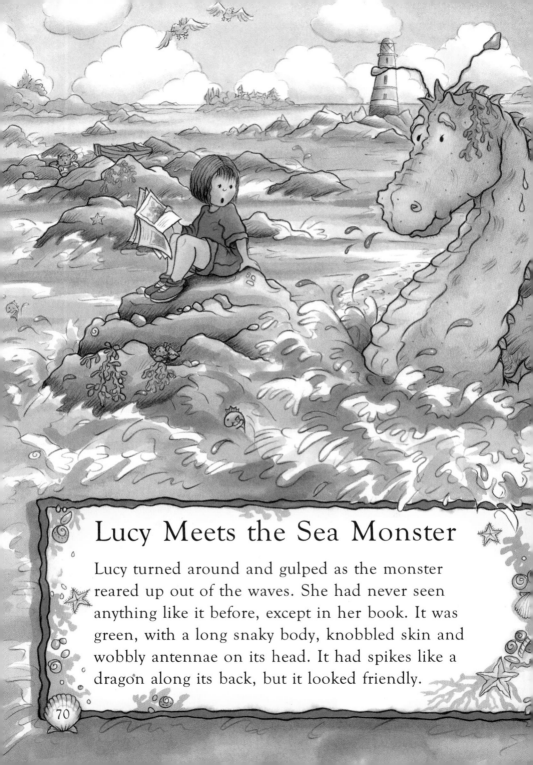

# Lucy Meets the Sea Monster

Lucy turned around and gulped as the monster reared up out of the waves. She had never seen anything like it before, except in her book. It was green, with a long snaky body, knobbled skin and wobbly antennae on its head. It had spikes like a dragon along its back, but it looked friendly.

Imagine Lucy's surprise when the strange creature began to speak.

"Hello," it said. "My name's Horace. I'm a sea monster."

"H . . . h . . . hello," stammered Lucy. "I'm Lucy and this is Tom Cat." But where WAS Tom Cat? He had vanished.

**Can you spot Tom Cat?**

71

# The Adventure Begins

"I must rescue Tom Cat!" Lucy exclaimed.

"I'll help you," said Horace. "Climb onto my back."

Lucy looked doubtfully at Horace's spikes, but when she touched one it was surprisingly soft. She jumped up and held on tightly. Horace's tail snaked from side to side and they whizzed away, whooshing through the waves.

A sleek silvery shape suddenly leapt up and dived quickly down again, but not before Lucy caught sight of a beady eye and a cheeky, friendly grin.

Dolphins!
There were lots of
them on all sides,
chattering and dancing around
Horace and Lucy.
"Have you seen my cat?" Lucy asked them.
"Try Blue Bird Island," one called, pushing a map
of the islands into Lucy's hand.

**Which one do you think is Blue Bird Island?**

# Blue Bird Island

"We're here," Horace said, cheerily.

Lucy jumped ashore on Blue Bird Island and heard the sounds of splashing and shouting nearby. She raced along the rocky beach and found some children tying up their boat. Lucy was aware of eyes watching in the distance, behind the trees.

There was no sign of Tom Cat here, but one of the children had seen him and the others gave her helpful directions. She had to find One Tree Island. Lucy stared at the islands across the bay.

**Can you find One Tree Island?**

The island has a tower on it . . .

. . . with a pointed turret, like a witch's hat . . .

. . . and no other buildings.

# Finn the Fishergirl

Horace zipped across to One Tree Island where they met a little fishergirl. She began to speak to them, but what she said was in rhyme.

*"Finn is my name*
*and if you'll help with my game,*
*I'll put you on track*
*to get your cat back."*

It was very puzzling, but slowly Lucy and Horace began to understand Finn. They agreed to help her with her game and in return, she told them what they must do to follow Tom Cat.

*"Through a maze made of coral that's the first thing to do.*
*The route through is tricky, but here is a clue:*
*look out for clear water, beware of sharp rocks,*
*watch out for the sharks and avoid any shocks.*

*Next stop is Shell Isle and there you must find
twelve shells shaped like starfish - the bright yellow kind.
Give these to old Toby, and he will quite soon
show you the way to the great Lost Lagoon.
And now for my game that you promised to play,
I can't play alone, I've been trying all day.
You must use your eyes and do as I bid -
find how many squids you can see here with Sid."*

A little squid wiggled a wavy
tentacle at Lucy. It was Sid, but
he was the only squid she could see.
Or was he?

**Can you find Sid? How
many other squids can
you see?**

# The Coral Maze

Horace and Lucy said goodbye and set off for the coral maze.

"It's not going to be easy to find a way through," Horace said when they arrived. "The coral is spiky and sharp and there are dangers lurking."

**The white flag marks the way out to the open sea. Can you find a way through the maze, steering clear of the spiky coral and lurking creatures?**

# Shell Isle

"Whew, I'm glad that's over," said Horace, when they reached the end of the coral maze. "Now let's go to Shell Isle to search for the shells for Toby."

Lucy gasped with astonishment when she saw Shell Isle. Everywhere she looked there were shells gleaming and glittering in the sunshine. There was a shell jetty, a hut made from shells and even a shell boat. The shells looked so pretty that Lucy began to collect them in a basket.

Then she remembered that she had to find some special shells.

Lucy darted up and down. She soon found the twelve yellow star shaped shells and they were ready to look for Toby at the gateway to the Lost Lagoon.

**Can you spot the twelve yellow star shells that Lucy needs?**

# The Lost Lagoon

When Lucy saw Toby she was speechless. He had a fishy tail!

"You're a merman!" she spluttered.

Toby smiled down at her over his glasses. He swished his scaly tail and counted his shells.

"You can go into the Lagoon now," he said.

They sailed on into the Lost Lagoon. At the far side, there were amazing tutti frutti trees growing along the banks.

Just as Lucy and Horace were wondering what to do next, a face popped out of the leaves.

"Hello, I'm Olivia, I study birds," she called. "I get a bird's eye view of the island from up here. I can help you find your furry friend ~ if you help me first. I'm trying to find the Golden Spotted Wonderbird. Its tail has five gold spotted feathers which curl up at the ends. If you can spot it for me, I'll tell you which way your cat went."

**Can you spot the Golden Spotted Wonderbird?**

# The Rainbow River

When Olivia saw the Wonderbird she almost fell out of her tree with excitement.

"Your cat went that way, along the Rainbow River," she pointed.

Lucy stared at the winding, whirling waterway. "It looks a bit choppy," she said.

Horace began to swim.
Waves whipped up as the river
rushed and swirled
hurrying them onward until . . .
Oh no! SPLASH!
SPLUTTER!

Lucy and Horace dived over the edge of a waterfall. Coughing and gasping they bobbed up to the surface again. The Rainbow River roared and raced along to the sea. Suddenly Lucy caught sight of something very familiar.

**What has Lucy spotted?**

# Under the Sea

Tom Cat whizzed around and around in a whirlpool,
spinning and sinking down below the waves.

"There's only one way for you to follow him," said
Horace, "And luckily help is at hand."

To Lucy's surprise, a small fish began gulping air. With
each gulp, the fish puffed up and grew bigger and bigger,
until it was enormous.

"It's a puffa fish," Horace told Lucy. "Sit very still."

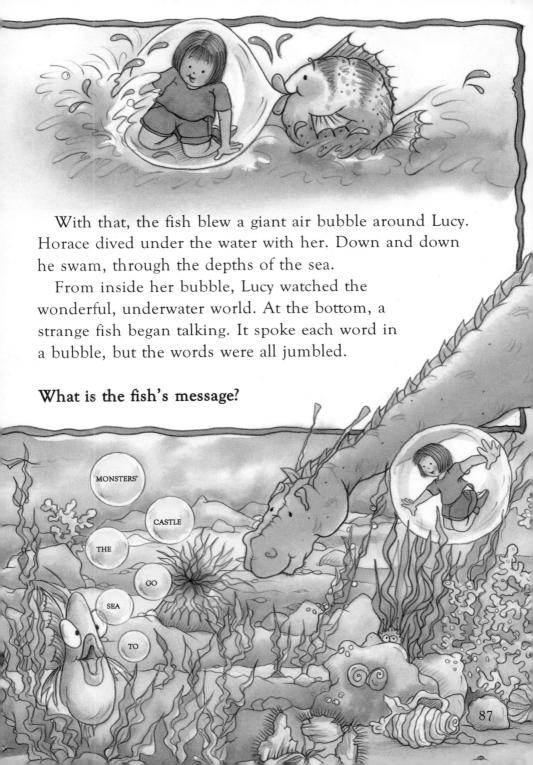

With that, the fish blew a giant air bubble around Lucy. Horace dived under the water with her. Down and down he swam, through the depths of the sea.

From inside her bubble, Lucy watched the wonderful, underwater world. At the bottom, a strange fish began talking. It spoke each word in a bubble, but the words were all jumbled.

**What is the fish's message?**

MONSTERS'

CASTLE

THE

GO

SEA

TO

# The Galleon

Lucy watched shimmering fish flash past. Two
turtles chased each other through coral arches and
waving weeds. The reeds rippled apart and Lucy
stared ahead into the black mouth of a
dark cave and tunnel.

Horace disappeared inside and Lucy followed. The
tunnel ended and Lucy blinked in surprise.
A splendid sunken galleon lay half-buried in the sand.
But Lucy couldn't see Horace anywhere.

**Where is Horace? Can you find him?**

# Horace's Home

"Hold tight," said Horace. "I have a surprise for you."

Lucy clung on to Horace's tail until suddenly she lost her grip. She bounced down and down, tumbling bumpety, bumpety, BUMP. She landed on soft sand and sat staring up at a fantastic fairytale castle.

"It's my home," said Horace. "And here are my family and friends. They all want to meet you but they're a bit shy."

Family? Friends? Lucy could only see fish and funny fishy monsters. But Horace explained that the sea monsters were the ones with two wobbly antennae on their heads.

**How many sea monsters do you think there are?**

# Surprise Party

Lucy followed Horace inside the castle. Her
bubble popped and she found she could
breathe without it. Horace introduced her to
all sorts of sea creatures and led her on to a
tall, arched doorway. The gleaming shell
doors slowly opened.

Lucy gazed at a sea of faces. The monsters and their friends were sitting at a long table in the longest room Lucy had ever seen. They all began to speak at once.

"We're having a party to celebrate your visit," said Nessie, Horace's sister. "Our other special guest is already here."

**Who is the other special guest?**

# Goodbye

Lucy gave Tom Cat a big hug and squeeze before she was whisked away to dance. The wonderful party passed in a whirl. Lucy ate and sang and danced . . . until suddenly it was time to go.

Lucy and Tom Cat climbed onto Horace's back and waved goodbye to their new friends. Almost before they knew it, they were back at the beach where their adventure had begun.

"I don't want to say goodbye to you, Horace," Lucy said, hugging him.

Horace smiled, "But I'll see you again very soon."

Lucy and Tom Cat jumped down onto the sandy shore and waved to Horace as he swam back to sea.

"Lucy!" called the familiar voice of her mother. "It's time for supper!"

# Answers

## Pages 68-69

A green sea monster is coming closer to Lucy's rock. It is circled in the picture.

## Pages 70-71

Tom Cat is being washed out to sea.

## Pages 72-73

Lucy decides that this must be Blue Bird Island. It is the only one with blue birds on it.

## Pages 74-75

This is One Tree Island. It has only one tree, a tower with a pointed turret and there are no other buildings on it.

## Pages 76-77

There are eleven little squids including Sid. You can see them all circled here in the picture.

This is Sid the Squid.

## Pages 78-79

Lucy's and Horace's way through the coral maze to the open sea is marked in black.

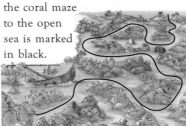

## Pages 80-81

You can see the twelve yellow star shaped shells that Lucy has to find circled here.

## Pages 82-83

This is the Golden Spotted Wonderbird. Can you see his five curly tail feathers?

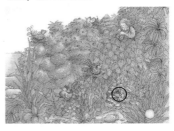

## Pages 84-85

Lucy has spotted Tom Cat. Here he is.

## Pages 86-87

When you put all the words in the right order, the fish's message is, "GO TO THE SEA MONSTERS' CASTLE."

## Pages 88-89

Here is Horace. He is well hidden behind the plants.

## Pages 90-91

You can see the ten sea monsters marked here.

## Pages 92-93

Did you spot the other special guest? It is Tom Cat.

# Wendy the Witch

Karen Dolby

Illustrated by Brenda Haw

# Contents

This is George and Lily and their granny, Wendy. Granny Wendy is just like anyone else's granny except that she looks a bit different. That's because she's learning to be a witch.

Granny Wendy has a problem. She hasn't been doing very well in her spellcraft classes and now she's been called in to see the Head Witch.

# In the Head's Office

Granny was in trouble. The Head Wizard was there as well as the Head Witch. This was serious.

"I'm afraid your spell work has not reached the mark," the Head Witch began.

"We know you try hard, but we can only give you one last chance," said the Head Wizard. "You will have to take a spell test tomorrow at 12 o'clock."

**TEST SPELLS**

1 Pull a rabbit from a cauldron.
2 Get your broomstick to hover.
3 Make someone invisible.
4 Find and perform your own special spell.

"Here are a list of the spells you must perform," the Head Wizard explained. "If you get them right you will become a proper witch at last. But if you fail, you will have to hand back your witch's hat and broomstick."

Granny hastily gathered her belongings. "Oops," she muttered.

In her hurry, she had dropped a vital piece of her witchy equipment.

**What had Granny Wendy dropped?**

# George's Good Idea

"Don't worry, Granny," said Lily, trying to cheer her up. "We'll help you with your spells."

"Start with the rabbit," George suggested, opening Granny Wendy's spellbook. "That looks easy enough."

Easy?

Not for Granny.

"As soon as she uttered the magic words there was a terrible smell and leaping frogs everywhere. But there was no sign of a rabbit.

"Perhaps you'll do better with your own special spell," said Lily hopefully.

"Mmmm," muttered Granny Wendy. "A special spell. If only I knew where to find one."

"What you need is a special spell book," said George. "Isn't there a library you can go to?"

"Of course. The Spell Library!" cried Granny Wendy. "What a brilliant idea, George. Now what did I do with my library card?" She turned out her pockets and rummaged through her bag, picked up the cat and checked under her hat. But the vital yellow card was nowhere to be found.

**Can you find the library card?**

# The Spell Library

Granny Wendy, George and Lily set off down the high street and across the square until they came to a building that looked just like a normal library.

George couldn't help feeling disappointed as he looked at the other people going inside. They looked so ordinary. "Are they really wizards and witches?" he asked. "You'd never guess."

"Every one of them," said Granny Wendy. "They're in disguise, you see."

Inside, there were lots of books with recipes for spells, but most were very complicated and not very special. Before long, Granny Wendy was looking cross-eyed and confused, but George had spotted something he thought might help.

**What has George found to help Granny?**

WHAT'S WHAT &
WHO'S WHO OF
WITCHCRAFT

OLD SPELLS FOR SALE.
The Olde Curiosity Shoppe,
Witch Way, Wandsworth.

GREEN FROGS and tiny
toads always in stock at
The Ponds, Green Witch, Common.

SLIPPERY SLIME Trick,
performed by me, one, &
only Misty Ease. Tel: 9556.

WITCH HAZEL—
will magic away your
warts. Cauldron Castle,
Spell City.

LOOKING FOR THAT
SPECIAL SPELL? Visit
the Great Wise Wizard.
Look for this sign.

105

# Star Flight

"Let's go!" cried George. "Let's visit the Great Wise Wizard! Maybe he'll give you a few witchy lessons too."

"I can't do that. He's famous. He's the cleverest wizard in the world." Granny Wendy looked shocked. But she really had nothing to lose. Maybe it was worth a try.

The Great Wise Wizard's castle was a long way away. "We'll have to fly there on my trusty broom," said Granny Wendy. "Jump up."

George and Lily were not too sure, especially when the broomstick wobbled wildly as they climbed aboard.

"Abracadabra, diddly-day," Granny chanted. "Take us to the Great Wise Wizz wa . . . Oops! I'm a little muddled."

Too late. The broomstick jolted up and down a few times then zoomed up into the sky. Distant stars rushed even closer.

"We're on the Great Wizzy Way," Granny exclaimed. "I don't know where to go from here. Maybe a signpost will help. Can you remember the sign we have to look for?"

**Which signpost should they follow?**

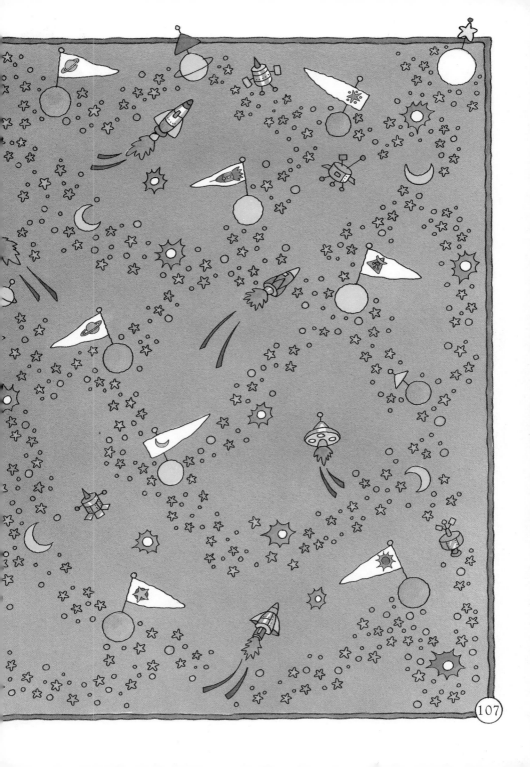

# Mysterious Map

The broomstick zoomed off
at lightning speed, skimming
stars, before it shot back down
to earth, crash-landing beside a
huge old boot.

"Must belong to a giant," said
Granny, picking herself up. "Oh
no, we're in trouble. My
broomstick is broken."

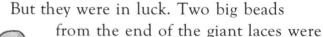

But they were in luck. Two big beads
from the end of the giant laces were
just what they needed to fix
the broomstick. "It's a bit
wobbly," said Granny. "But
I think it'll work. Now,
where are we?"

As if in answer, a large bird
appeared and hovered just above
their heads. It held a scroll of paper
in its beak. George caught a
glowing glass ball, like a giant
marble, that fell from the scroll.
Granny unrolled it to discover
a picture map.

"A mountain with a big boot on top!" Granny
exclaimed. "That's where we are. And look, there's
the Wise Wizard's sign. He must live there."
"Perhaps he sent us the map," said Lily.
"Could he know we're on our way?"
George looked at the glowing
marble and had a funny feeling they
were being watched. And he was
right. The Great Wise Wizard was
keeping a close eye on them.

**Which is the mountain where the
Great Wise Wizard lives?**

# Mountain Maze

George tucked the giant marble into his pocket and they set off. Lily kept watch for giants and held on tightly. The broomstick jolted even more than usual and didn't feel very safe.

It was a bumpy ride, but they were soon preparing to land at the bottom of the mountain where the Great Wise Wizard lived.

"We have to get to the entrance at the top of the mountain," said Granny Wendy. "But my broomstick is too wobbly. We'd better walk instead. It looks quite tricky and we'll have to steer clear of those red monsters. They don't look very friendly."

**Can you find a way to the entrance at the top of the mountain?**

# Ice Cavern

They stepped through the entrance at the top of the mountain and were amazed to find themselves inside a glistening ice cavern which sparkled like diamonds.

"I can see a castle," exclaimed George. "That must be where the Wizard lives."

George ran two paces and fell sprawling on the slippery, glassy floor. Lily helped him to his feet and slowly they made their way up to the castle.

**Can you find your way along the paths to the castle?**

# The Key to the Castle

The castle towered above them.
"I wonder how we get in?"
Granny pondered.
There were four doors in the
weird rocks in front of them.
Perhaps one of these was the way in?
Lily tried but all were locked.
Again George had the
eerie feeling they were
being watched. In his
pocket the giant
marble was
getting hot.

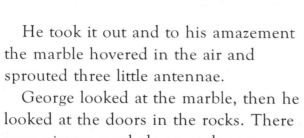

He took it out and to his amazement the marble hovered in the air and sprouted three little antennae.

George looked at the marble, then he looked at the doors in the rocks. There were picture symbols on each one. Suddenly he had a brilliant idea. If he slotted the marble into one of the pictures it would make the sign of the Great Wise Wizard. Of course! The marble was a magic key.

**Do you know which door it will open?**

# Inside the Castle

When the door creaked open they did not know what to expect, but certainly not the sunny garden that lay before them. They stepped down into a courtyard and only then saw a gardener holding a sad-looking pig in his arms.

Granny Wendy took one look at the poor little piglet and the half-eaten rhubarb leaf and guessed the problem. She rummaged in her pockets and whisked out a bottle of medicine.

"Three drops of this and he'll soon be fit," she said. The mixture worked like magic and the piglet happily trotted off to find his friends. The man looked impressed. Granny gave him the rest of the bottle. "Never more than three drops a day," she said.

"Cool," George whispered to Lily. Granny Wendy might have trouble with her spells, but she was a whiz with animals and plants. "Now where's the Wizard?"

"I think we've already found him," said Lily. "Though he's not quite what I expected."

"Don't be silly," said George. "Wizards don't look like that. He's the gardener, isn't he?"

**What do you think?**
**Could he be the Great Wise Wizard?**

# The Book of Special Spells

There was a puff of smoke and the man stood transformed, looking much more like a Great Wise Wizard should.

"Visitors! How nice," he exclaimed. "No one's been here since two years last Tuesday."

The Wizard led the way inside his castle. "Please call me Douglas. All my friends do . . . it's my name, you know."

Soon they were standing inside a vast chamber. "Thank you for helping my pig," said Douglas. "Now perhaps I can help you. Let me fix this for a start."

Before their very eyes, the broomstick became whole again. "The secret of successful broomstickery is to get your magic words right," he smiled.

"That . . . and a little wizard dust." He sprinkled something sparkly onto the broom.

Then he magicked up a wizard snack for Lily and George and led Granny off to give her a few tips for her spell test.

The Wizard's tips were just what Granny Wendy needed. Her broomstick hovered in the air without so much as a shake or wobble.

"With a little practice, you'll be as good as any witch I know," Douglas said.

Then he unlocked a cupboard and took out a dusty old book. "My book of special spells," he said. "Why not try this one." He pointed to an open page. "But you'll have to decipher it yourself."

Granny Wendy looked puzzled for a moment. Then Lily saw Douglas sprinkle a little dust onto Granny's hat and at once, Granny smiled. "I've got it!" she exclaimed.

**Can you decipher the spell?**

:gloop golden of
cup a and corn
of handfuls three
with Mix. acorn
magic a and
toadstool spotted
red a: flower

shaped bell-blue
a; teeth dragon's
two; cobweb one
Take: egg golden
a lay to goose
your get to
spell special

119

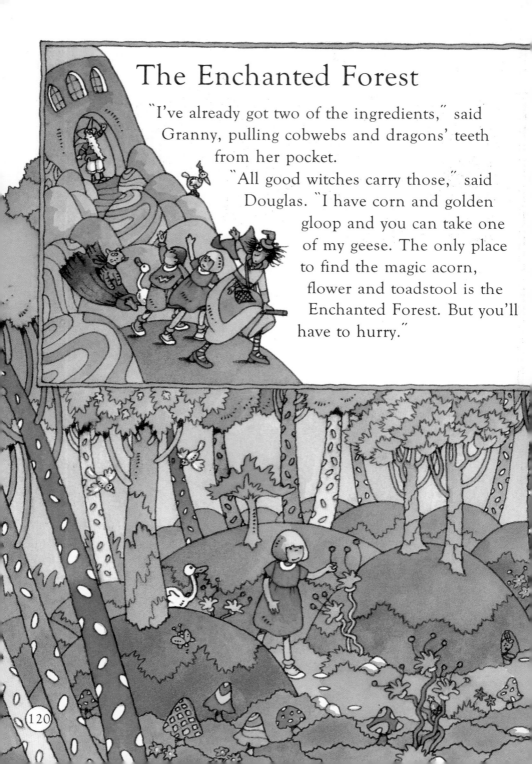

# The Enchanted Forest

"I've already got two of the ingredients," said Granny, pulling cobwebs and dragons' teeth from her pocket.

"All good witches carry those," said Douglas. "I have corn and golden gloop and you can take one of my geese. The only place to find the magic acorn, flower and toadstool is the Enchanted Forest. But you'll have to hurry."

They said goodbye and set off smoothly on the broomstick.

They found the Enchanted Forest. It was a strange place. Wild animal calls rang out and curious plants grew everywhere. George and Lily would have liked to explore but they had no time. The toadstool was easy to spot, but the flower and acorn were more tricky.

**Can you find them?**

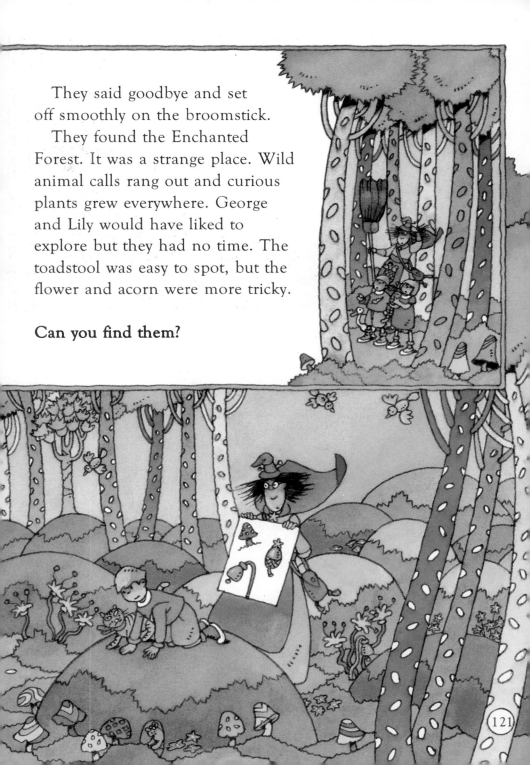

# Lift Off!

At last, Granny Wendy had everything she needed but it was now nearly time for the spell test.

"Come on Granny," cried Lily as they leaped onto the broomstick. "We can do it."

The broomstick seemed to have a mind of its own, zooming along at breakneck speed, looping the loop and skimming the clouds.

Lily remembered the powder Douglas had sprinkled over it and wondered if that had anything to do with it. "We're supersonic," she gasped as they overtook a jet.

The broomstick dived earthwards, skidding to a stop as the clock struck twelve. Granny straightened her hat. She tucked the goose under her arm and gulped. This was it. Time for her test. But there was a surprise in store for her when she saw the panel of testers.

**Do you recognize anyone?**

# Granny's Test

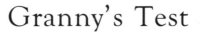

The test began. Nervously, Granny Wendy mixed the ingredients for her special spell and set them to simmer while she carried on with the other tasks. First she pulled a fluffy rabbit out of her cauldron, then her broomstick hovered perfectly.

Next, she uttered the magic words to make George invisible. This was quite tricky and at first nothing happened. Granny said the words again. Still nothing. She tried again.

This time Granny concentrated so hard that her hat suddenly took off. It whizzed into orbit around the room which was lucky as George had almost but not quite disappeared.

Lily jumped in to hide what was left of him while everyone else watched the whizzing hat ~ all except Douglas who giggled.

Granny was worn out by her efforts. Now all that was left was to try out her special mix on the goose. Would it work? There was silence. Everyone waited. Time ticked on until the goose hiccuped and there it was. The goose was sitting on a golden egg.

Everyone gazed at the golden egg, so no one noticed two shoes tiptoe behind the table. George was still almost invisible and he wanted to check Granny's marks. She needed 25 to pass.

**Has Granny made it? How many marks has she got?**

# Granny Gets it Right

Granny Wendy could hardly believe it. She had passed her test. Now she could keep her hat and broomstick. Best of all she was a real witch at last.

Granny jumped for joy. "Come on," she called to George and Lily. "I'll take you for a celebratory spin on my broomstick."

They were about to set off when a familiar figure came bounding down the school steps, waving wildly. "Wait for me!" yelled Douglas. "I don't want to miss all the fun. I'm coming too."

# Answers

### Pages 100-101
Granny has dropped her spell book. It is circled below.

### Pages 102-103
The Spell Library card is circled below.

### Pages 104-105
George has spotted something in the open book. It says that if you need a special spell you should visit the Great Wise Wizard.

### Pages 106-107
The signpost they should follow is circled below. It's the only one with Wizard's sign on it.

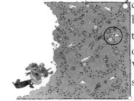

### Pages 108-109
The mountain where the Great Wise Wizard lives is circled below.

### Pages 110-111
The way to the entrance at the top of the mountain is marked here.

## Pages 112-113

The way along the
paths to the castle
is marked here.

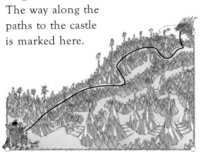

## Pages 114-115

The key will open the door circled
below. The glass ball fits the
carving on it to make the Great
Wise Wizard's sign.

## Pages 116-117

The man is
indeed the Great
Wise Wizard.
We know this
because he has
the Wizard's
symbol on his
pocket. It is
circled here.

## Pages 118-119

The spell is written the wrong way around.
Start at the bottom of the right-hand page
and read up. Then go onto the bottom of the
left-hand page and read up. It says:
*To get your goose to lay a golden egg: Take
one cobweb, two dragon's teeth, a blue bell-
shaped flower, a red spotted toadstool and a
magic acorn. Mix with three handfuls of corn
and a cup of golden gloop.*

## Pages 120-121

The toadstool, the
flower and the acorn
are circled below.

## Pages 122-123

The Great Wise
Wizard is one of the
judges. He is the
one in the middle.
The Head Wizard
and Head Witch are there too.

## Pages 124-125

Granny has 27 marks, so
she has passed the test.

This edition first published in 2004 by Usborne
Publishing Ltd., Usborne House, 83-85 Saffron Hill,
London EC1N 8RT, England. www.usborne.com
Copyright © 2004, 2002, 1995, 1994 Usborne
Publishing Ltd. The name Usborne and the
devices ♈ ⊕ are Trade Marks of Usborne
Publishing Ltd. All rights reserved.